Not Bartlett's

THOUGHTS ON THE
PLEASURES OF LIFE:
PEOPLE, LOVE, GARDENS,
DOGS, AND MORE

✀

EDITED BY

ELISE LUFKIN

HELEN MARX BOOKS

ART BY JENNIFER GALPIN-MIKESH

The publisher would like to thank the
authors, publishers, and literary representatives
listed on pages 141–142 for permission to reprint
from copyrighted and previously published material.

AUTHOR'S NOTE

Since reading has so greatly enhanced my life,
I will donate all royalties from *Not Bartlett's* to
First Book, an organization that promotes literacy by
giving books to children from low-income families.

TO MY PARENTS
WHO READ ALOUD WITH
CONTAGIOUS ENTHUSIASM
AND INSTILLED IN ME
A SENSE OF THE PLEASURES
TO BE FOUND IN BOOKS.

ACKNOWLEDGMENTS

I am grateful to Helen Marx of Helen Marx Books for her encouragement and advice, as well as for her help in making this project a reality. Also, I would like to thank Colleen Daly for her invaluable contributions in editing and source research, Jonathan Rabinowitz for sharing his creativity and wit, and Laurie Leman for her patience, perseverance, and skill in keeping everything straight.

CONTENTS

Introduction

All my life I have loved to read. I am intrigued by words and especially by the way in which different words in different combinations can evoke such vivid impressions and images. Mark Twain points out that "The difference between the right word and the almost right word is the difference between lightning and the lightning bug."

When I read, I look for passages that resonate, passages that make me say to myself, "Yes, I know that," or "Yes, but I had not thought of it from that angle," or simply, "Wow!" For years I have scribbled down the bits and pieces that appealed to me. The drawer in my bedside table is overflowing with scraps of paper, notes of those bits and pieces, many of which have found their way into this book. I'm afraid I was not always careful to note the source of each quotation; often I can give only the author.

Of course, I am still collecting; it is impossible for me to stop. To quote Nicolas Chamfort, "Most collectors of verses and sayings proceed as if they were eating cherries or oysters, choosing the best first, and ending by eating them all."

Family

⸎ ⸎ Families are petri dishes, producing all kinds of emotions. ⸎ ⸎ ⸎ ⸎

Indeed she herself was accustomed to think that entire freedom from the necessity of behaving agreeably was included in the Almighty's intentions about families.

GEORGE ELIOT, *Middlemarch*

—

Fond as we are of our loved ones, there comes at times during their absence an unexplained peace.

ANNE SHAW

—

You feel yourself at times in danger of thinking meanly of the human personality; numerosity, as it were, swallows up quality, and the perpetual sense of other elbows and knees begets a yearning for the desert.

HENRY JAMES, *English Hours*

—

They had already begun to weave a thicker clothing of family kindness against the chill of bereavement.

SYLVIA TOWNSEND WARNER, *Lolly Willowes*

Family

A thought on death — I can reconcile myself to believing in a time when I shall not make tea, listen to Bach, etc.; but scarcely to a time when no one will. I suppose this is why one wants an heir . . . it is a grateful response to all the things one has loved. "Here is someone to go on loving you," one would hope to say.

The Diaries of Sylvia Townsend Warner

—

Hold your parents tenderly, for the world will seem a strange and lonely place when they're gone.

WILLIAM LUCE, *The Belle of Amherst*

—

Often, in old age, they [the sisters] become each other's chosen and most happy companions. In addition to their shared memories of childhood and their relationship to each other's children, they . . . carry the echoes of their mother's voice.

MARGARET MEAD,
Blackberry Winter

Family

I am quite sure that to be fearless is the first requisite for a woman; everything else that is good will grow naturally out of that, as a tree has leaves and fruit and grows tall and full provided its roots have a good hold of the ground. Bring her up to be fearless and unintimidated by frowns, hints and conventions, and then she will be full of mercy and grace and generosity. *Letters: Sylvia Townsend Warner*

The only thing to do with family skeletons is to take them out of the closet and dance with them.

Author unknown

It is in the shelter of each other that the people live.

Irish proverb

Home is the place where, when you have to go there,
They have to take you in.

ROBERT FROST, from
"The Death of the Hired Man"

Family

Friends and Others

Friendship provides much comfort and joy in our lives. Dealing with those to whom we are indifferent or even actually dislike (my mother strongly disapproved of the word "hate") is certainly not a joy; it is, however, invariably interesting.

At twenty, we find our friends for ourselves, but it takes
Heaven to find us one when we are fifty-seven.

W. H. AUDEN

The French *seem*, which is all that matters, to love one
so much. NANCY MITFORD,
letter to Evelyn Waugh

Whom we love best, to them we can say the least.

JOHN RAY

The real marriage of true minds is for any two people to
possess a sense of humor or irony pitched in exactly the
same key, so that their joint glances at any subject cross
like interarching search lights.

EDITH WHARTON, letter to Henry James,
in *A Backward Glance*

Both of us thought our arguments incontrovertible,
and neither of us changed our minds in the least.

The Diaries of Sylvia Townsend Warner

Friends and Others

It was not, in the end, enough to be a Woman With a Secret, if to one's friends one appeared to be a woman without a secret.   MARY MCCARTHY,
Cruel and Barbarous Treatment

The apologetic politeness I always feel with people I do not really like . . .   LAWRENCE DURRELL, *Justine*

I am not a vengeful woman . . . possibly for the perfectly working reason that if you just sit back and wait, the bastards will get theirs without your doing anything about it, and it will be fancier than anything you could have dreamed up.   DOROTHY PARKER

[She seemed like] a tall lighthouse sending out kindly beams which some took for welcome instead of warnings against the rocks.   MURIEL SPARK,
"The Curtain Blown by the Breeze"

Friends and Others

Women do not leave situations like this: we push up our sleeves, lean in closer, and say, "What do you need? Tell me what you need and by God I will do it." I believe that the souls of women flatten and anchor themselves in times of adversity, lay in for the stay.

ELIZABETH BERG, *Talk Before Sleep*

One is so apt to think of people's affection as a fixed quantity, instead of a sort of moving sea with the tide always going out or coming in but still fundamentally there. I believe this difficulty in making allowance for the tide is the reason for half the broken friendships.

FREYA STARK, letter

It was a delightful visit; perfect, in being much too short.

JANE AUSTEN, *Emma*

And the song, from beginning to end,
I found again in the heart of a friend.

HENRY WADSWORTH LONGFELLOW,
from "The Arrow and the Song"

Friends and Others

Love and Lovers

ᦊ The subject of love is endlessly fascinating and endlessly varied. I am fortunate enough to have known love in many forms: euphoric new love, the steady comfort and delight of seasoned love, struggles with love, the heartbreaking sadness of lost love. I have enjoyed many writers' slants on this universally engaging topic. ᦊ

In the impetuous arrogance of new love, I decided there
were no obstacles we could not overcome.

ISABEL ALLENDE, *Paula*

While up from my heart's root
So great a sweetness flows
I shake from head to foot.

WILLIAM BUTLER YEATS,
from "Friends"

In the snow light
In the swan light
In the white-on-white light
Of a winter storm,
My delight and your delight
Kept each other warm.

MAY SARTON,
from "The Snow Light"

Love and Lovers

It is something—it can be everything—to have found a fellow bird with whom you can sit among the rafters while the drinking and boasting and reciting and fighting go on below; a fellow bird whom you can look after and find bugs and seeds for; one who will patch your bruises and straighten your ruffled feathers and mourn over your hurts when you accidentally fly into something you can't handle.

WALLACE STEGNER, *The Spectator Bird*

All in green went my love riding
on a great horse of gold
into the silver dawn.

E. E. CUMMINGS, from
"All in green went my love riding"

Rise up, my love, my fair one, and come away. For, lo! the winter is past, the rain is over and gone; the flowers appear on the earth.   Song of Solomon

Love and Lovers

Water may be older than light, diamonds crack in hot goat's blood, mountain tops give off cold fire, it may happen that a crab is caught with the shadow of a hand on its back, that the wind be imprisoned in a bit of knotted string. And it may be that love sometimes occurs without pain or misery.

ANNIE PROULX,
The Shipping News

~

Most things break, including hearts. The lessons of a life amount not to wisdom but to scar tissue and callus.

WALLACE STEGNER,
The Spectator Bird

~

They wept for the love that something incurably naughty and childish in them made them destroy; and they looked into the gray years ahead of them, which they must spend imprisoned in their freedom from each other.

REBECCA WEST

Love and Lovers

I would not want; I would not ask. And it has gotten one, not safety and certainty, but—nothing.

JANE LECOMPTE,
Moon Passage

What scalpel can unknot love at the bone?

MAY SARTON

> You left me, sweet, two legacies,—
> A legacy of love
> A Heavenly Father would content,
> Had He the offer of;
>
> You left me boundaries of pain
> Capacious as the sea,
> Between eternity and time,
> Your consciousness and me.

EMILY DICKINSON, "Bequest"

Love and Lovers

Go I must along my ways
  Though my heart be ragged,
Dripping bitter through the days
  Festering, and jagged.
Smile I must at every twinge,
  Kiss, to time its throbbing;
He that tears a heart to fringe
  Hates the noise of sobbing.

DOROTHY PARKER,
from "The Second Oldest Story"

It does not astonish or make us angry that it takes a whole
year to bring into the house three great white peonies and
two pale blue iris. It seems altogether right and appropriate
that these glories are earned with long patience and faith
. . . and also that it is altogether right and appropriate that
they cannot last. Yet in our human relations we are outraged
when the supreme moments, the moments of flowering, must
be waited for . . . and then cannot last. We reach a summit
and then have to go down again.

MAY SARTON, *Journal of a Solitude*

Love and Lovers

Love and death are the two great gifts that we pass on;
and usually they are passed on unopened.

RAINER MARIA RILKE

Who would have thought my shrivell'd heart
Could have recover'd greenness? It was gone
Quite under ground . . .

GEORGE HERBERT, from "The Flower"

Love and its transforming power have laid out a far more
generous future than the one for which he had been willing
to settle.
CAROL SHIELDS, *The Stone Diaries*

But true love is a durable fire,
In the mind ever burning,
Never sick, never dead, never cold,
From itself never turning.

SIR WALTER RALEGH, from
"As You Came from the Holy Land"

Love and Lovers

There is something about love — I will not say defective for the defect lies in ourselves: but something we have mistaken about its nature. For example, the love you now feel for Justine is not a different love for a different object but the same love you feel for Melissa trying to work itself out through the medium of Justine. Love is horribly stable, and each of us is only allotted a certain portion of it, a ration. It is capable of appearing in an infinity of forms and attaching itself to an infinity of people. But it is limited in quantity, can be used up, become shop-worn and faded before it reaches its true object. For its destination lies somewhere in the deepest regions of the psyche where it will come to recognize itself as self-love, the ground upon which we build the sort of health of the psyche. I do not mean egoism or narcissism.

LAWRENCE DURRELL, *Justine*

People don't make commitments. They wake up one day to find them made.   PETER FEIBLEMAN, *Lilly*

Love and Lovers

She was always trying to be what her husband wished,
and never able to repose on his delight in what she was.

GEORGE ELIOT, *Middlemarch*

⚊

I say it with my true heart, the worst injury one can do to the
person who loves one is to cover oneself from head to foot in
a shining impenetrable condom of irreproachable behavior.

Letters: Sylvia Townsend Warner

⚊

Marrying a woman for her beauty makes no more sense
than eating a bird for its singing. But it's a common mistake
nonetheless.   CHARLES FRAZIER, *Cold Mountain*

⚊

After a blow in your life, don't buy real estate, don't sell real
estate, and don't marry Frank Sinatra.

Popular wisdom

Love and Lovers

"Set the table and sweep the floor —
Love will not come back to this door.

Plant your bulbs, sow summer flowers.
These be your joys, these your powers.

A cat for comfort, wood to burn,
And changing light as seasons turn.

Long hours alone and work to do —
These are your strength. These are for you."

So spoke myself. I listened well;
I thought that self had truth to tell.

But love came back after many a year,
Love all unasked knocked at the door,

Love all unasked broke down the door,
To bring me pain as it did before,

Love and Lovers

To bring me back lost poetry,
And all I'd meant alone to be.

What does myself now say to me?
"Open the door to Mystery.

Gather the grapes from any vine,
And make rich wine, and make rich wine,

Out of the passion comes the form,
And only passion keeps it warm.

Set the table, sweep the floor —
Forget the lies you told before."

MAY SARTON,
"Myself to Me"

Love and Lovers

Gardening

I come from a family of gardeners; my mother, her mother and her uncle, all four of my sisters, and all four of my daughters are gardeners, good gardeners. Even my two-year-old twin grandsons and their six-year-old big brother enjoy messing about in the dirt. Many of my friends are gardeners. I love reading about gardens and gardening, learning and fantasizing.

A garden is like those pernicious machineries which catch
a man's coat-skirt or his hand, and draw in his arm, his leg,
and his whole body to irresistible destruction.

RALPH WALDO EMERSON,
The Conduct of Life

I have particular friends whom I think of as gardening
friends, rather as though you shared a drink or a drug habit.

PENELOPE LIVELY,
in the magazine
Gardens Illustrated

> Great and beautiful is the world,
> Yet, how I do thank heaven
> That a small garden enclosed,
> I can call my own.

JOHANN WOLFGANG VON GOETHE

Gardening

It is agreeable to waddle about in one's own paradise, knowing that thousands of others have better gardens with better thises and thats, and better grown too, and no weeds at all. To know this and to grin as complacently as a terrier who just got into the deviled eggs, and to reflect that there is no garden in England or France I envy and not one I'd swap for mine: this is the aim of gardening—not to make us complacent idiots, exactly, but to make us content and calm for a time, with sufficient energy (even after wars with bindweed) to feel an awestruck thanks to God that such happiness can exist. For a few days, of course.

HENRY MITCHELL, *One Man's Garden*

What was Paradise?—but a Garden, an Orchard of Trees and Herbs, full of pleasure, and nothing there but delights.

WILLIAM LAWSON, *A New Orchard and Garden*, 1618

And now that I am rich with still another spring . . .

FLORENCE BELLIS, *Gardening and Beyond*

Gardening

Gardening is not a rational act. What matters is the immersion of the hands in the earth, that ancient ceremony of which the Pope kissing the tarmac is merely a pallid vestigial remnant. In the spring, at the end of the day, you should smell like dirt.

MARGARET ATWOOD, "Unearthing Suite"

Comparatively, our gardening is on a petty scale, — the gardener still nursing a few asters amid dead weeds, ignorant of the gigantic asters and roses which, as it were, overshadow him, and ask for none of his care . . . Why not take a more elevated and broader view, walk in the great garden; not skulk in a little debauched nook of it? Consider the beauty of the forest and not merely of a few impounded herbs.

HENRY DAVID THOREAU, "Autumn Tints"

The very works of, and in an Orchard or Garden are better than the ease and rest from other labours.

WILLIAM LAWSON, *A New Orchard and Garden*, 1618

Gardening

I worked out anguish in a garden.
Without the flowers,
The shadow of trees on snow, their punctuation,
I might not have survived.

MAY SARTON, from
"Gestalt at Sixty"

The hollyhocks are eight feet high and have been intermar-
rying since I first got them, and now have hit off some very
fine imitations of Rome: apricot tawnies and burned milk,
and one, just the color of Tiber mud.

Letters: Sylvia Townsend Warner

The longer I live the greater is my respect and affection
for manure in all its forms.

ELIZABETH VON ARNIM,
Elizabeth and Her German Garden

Gardening

It has taken me half a lifetime merely to find out what
is best worth doing, and a good slice out of another half
to puzzle out the ways of doing it.

GERTRUDE JEKYLL,
Colour Schemes for the Flower Garden

—

The true meaning of life is to plant trees, under whose shade
you do not expect to sit.   NELSON HENDERSON

—

For the last 40 years of my life I have broken my back,
my fingernails, and sometimes my heart, in the practical
pursuit of my favorite occupation.

VITA SACKVILLE-WEST, in an *Observer* article, 1958

—

What better way to get over a black mood than an hour
of furious weeding! That violent tearing up and casting
away of the dreadfully healthy weeds also tears up and
casts away the dreadfully healthy demons.   MAY SARTON

Gardening

All my hurts my garden spade can heal.

RALPH WALDO EMERSON,
from "Musketaquid"

In his wild-wood garden Jasper stayed late that evening,
subduing and cutting into the thickets of encroaching briars.
He very much enjoyed the work; delightful to slice below
the woody knot from which the felons sprouted. It was a
destruction of personal dislikes, and at the same time a
ransom for objects he considered precious.

MOLLY KEANE,
Time After Time

Things built come before things planted, and are more
important.

Sixteenth-century
Italian garden architect

Gardening

Because gardens are composed from living material, they cannot be preserved in the same way as buildings, paintings, furniture and costumes. The restorer may therefore have a sense not only of period but also of time sequences, from seasonal changes to the changes which occur within the time scale of trees and, too, of changing climates and micro-climates, and also a wide knowledge of maintenance problems and land and garden management.

Though gardens cannot remain static and frozen examples of the art of a period, yet the ideas which these gardens expressed should be understood, respected, interpreted and re-expressed. Ideas are in general external and are indeed the only reality.   H.F. CLARK, "The Restoration and
Reclamation of Gardens," Occasional
Paper for the Garden History Society

—

People's gardens are apt to die with them, even if the status quo is kept—or perhaps just because of that.
          EDDY SACKVILLE-WEST, writing about his cousin
Vita's famous garden at Sissinghurst after her death

Gardening

The central pleasure of gardening is that much of it goes on in the head—anticipation and creative day-dreaming, and above all those outbreaks of unbridled lust. Must have a dorycnium—not next week—instantly. How can I lay my hands on one of those strawberry ice cream coloured foxgloves? I spend hours poring over catalogs in a state of beady-eyed acquisitiveness.

PENELOPE LIVELY, in the magazine *Gardens Illustrated*

A severely truncated view of gardening, a dangerous view that suggests that the rewards of gardening are all in the achievement, when, in fact, most are in the striving.

GEORGE WATERS, in the magazine *Pacific Horticulture*

Come into the garden, Maud,
For the black bat, Night, has flown,
Come into the garden, Maud,
I am here at the gate alone.

ALFRED, LORD TENNYSON,
from "Maud—A Monodrama"

Gardening

People from another planet without flowers would think we must be mad with joy the whole time to have such things about us.

IRIS MURDOCH,
A Fairly Honorable Defeat

—

I love cruising other people's gardens. You can marvel, poach ideas or be satisfyingly dismissive.

PENELOPE LIVELY,
in the magazine *Gardens Illustrated*

—

Like most gardeners, I have an abiding mistrust of progress.

THOMAS CHRISTOPHER,
In Search of Lost Roses

Gardening

Now I feel as well as understand the impulse to lilacs
that moved the pioneers, now know that it was more
than simply wanting to have lilacs when they got there.
You take fuller possession of new ground when you grow
old plants in it, prove to your heart that you too can thrive
on unfamiliar soil. LESLIE LAND,
The 3000 Mile Garden

Gardening gives me back a sense of proportion about
everything except itself.

MAY SARTON,
Plant Dreaming Deep

Gardening

Dogs and a Cat or Two

Dogs have filled my life with love and delight. Here are some thoughts from others about these creatures, longtime companions for us. And let's not forget cats!

Brothers and Sisters, I bid you beware
Of giving your heart to a dog to tear.

RUDYARD KIPLING, from
"The Power of the Dog"

~

Scratch a dog and you'll find a permanent job.

FRANKLIN P. JONES

~

Dogs feel very strongly that they should always go with
you in the car, in case the need should arise for them to
bark violently at nothing right in your ear.

DAVE BARRY

Dogs and

No one who has not, upon returning from any absence, long or short, been greeted by a loving dog can understand what devotion is. There is no affection like it available anywhere on earth, and those for whom it is the heart's balm, as it is for me, understand what a love elixir is.

CAROLYN G. HEILBRUN, The Last Gift of Time

I would like to begin with, to say that though parents, husbands, children, lovers and friends are all very well, they are not dogs. In my day and turn having been each of the above,—except that instead of husbands I was wives,—I know what I am talking about, and am well acquainted with the ups and downs and sometimes almost hourly ones in the thin-skinned which seem inevitably to accompany human loves. Dogs are free from these fluctuations. Once they love, they love steadily, unchangingly, till their last breath. That is how I like to be loved. Therefore I will write of dogs.

ELIZABETH VON ARNIM, All the Dogs of My Life

a Cat or Two

He is your friend, your partner, your defender, your dog.
You are his life, his love, his leader. He will be yours, faithful
and true, to the last beat of his heart. You owe it to him
to be worthy of such devotion.

Author unknown

When we take the time and energy necessary to raise our
puppies correctly, when we learn to truly listen to them,
seeing them as they really are and guiding their development
accordingly, a deeper part of ourselves is unlocked, a part
more compassionate and less arrogant, more willing to share
life with another life. And whenever that happens, we know
the real meaning of happiness.

THE MONKS OF NEW SKETE,
The Art of Raising a Puppy

Freud wrote to a friend that dogs give people an opportu-
nity to give affection without ambivalence and a chance
to admire a life free from the almost unbearable conflicts
of civilization.

Dogs

The prophet Mohammed said that a man who never prayed his whole life would go to heaven because he once was kind to a starving cat.

—

Until one has loved an animal, a part of one's soul remains unawakened.   ANATOLE FRANCE

—

Newfoundland dogs are good to save children from drowning but you must have a pond of water handy and a child, or else there will be no profit in boarding a Newfoundland.   JOSH BILLINGS

—

A long pillow of purrs along my back.
                    MAY SARTON, from "Wilderness Lost,"
                    describing Bramble, her cat

Dogs and

A dog is the only exercise machine you cannot decide
to skip when you don't feel like it.

CAROLYN G. HEILBRUN,
The Last Gift of Time

 . . . Beauty without Vanity,
 Strength without Insolence,
 Courage without Ferocity,
 and all the Virtues of Man without his Vices.

LORD BYRON, on the death of
his beloved dog Boatswain

Don't accept your dog's admiration as conclusive evidence
that you are wonderful. ANN LANDERS

a Cat or Two

Writing and Reading

Writing is a challenge approached in various ways. Writers writing about writing can be fascinating, especially to a reader. Reading has entertained me, instructed me, and broadened my horizon.

The problem with fiction is that it must seem credible, while reality seldom is.   ISABEL ALLENDE, *Paula*

Writers begin as bewitched readers.

SUSAN SONTAG

[Writing is] like being harnessed to a shark.

VIRGINIA WOOLF, *The Diaries*
of Virginia Woolf, vol. 4

A poem . . . begins as a lump in the throat, a sense of wrong, a homesickness, a lovesickness. . . . It finds the thought and the thought finds the words.

ROBERT FROST, *The Letters of Robert Frost*
to Louis Untermeyer

Writing and Reading

Lawrence Durrell compares writing a poem to "trying to catch a lizard without its tail falling off."

"The Art of Fiction No. 23,"
Paris Review interview, 1959

In order to breathe, he must break all the windows.

VIRGINIA WOOLF, about James Joyce

The megalomaniac pleasure of creation . . . produces a type of elation which cannot be compared with that experienced by other mortals.   EDMUND BERGLER, "Can the Writer 'Resign' from His Calling?"

Biography lends to death a fresh horror.

OSCAR WILDE, "A Cheap Edition of a Great Man [Rossetti]"

Writing and Reading

Immature poets imitate; mature poets steal.

T. S. ELIOT, "Philip Massinger," in
The Sacred Wood: Essays on Poetry and Criticism

—

I realized that what interests me most is very different
characters grating their edges together.

ANNE TYLER, *New York Times* interview

—

My novels are based on the fantastic designs made by real
human beings earnestly laboring to maladjust themselves
to fate. . . . My characters are not slaves to an author's
propaganda. I give them their heads. They furnish their
own nooses.

DAWN POWELL, *Selected Letters of
Dawn Powell, 1913–1965*

—

If a writer has to rob his mother, he will not hesitate; the
"Ode on a Grecian Urn" is worth any number of old ladies.

WILLIAM FAULKNER, in *Writers at Work:
The Paris Review Interviews, 1959*

Writing and Reading

Yet when I wrote, the full facts were not at my disposal.
The picture I drew was a provisional one—like the picture
of a lost civilization deduced from a few fragmented vases,
an inscribed tablet, an amulet, some human bones, a gold
smiling death-mask.   LAWRENCE DURRELL, *Balthazar*

The difference between the right word and the almost
right word is the difference between lightning and the
lightning bug.   MARK TWAIN, letter, October 15, 1888

Words are nets through which all truth escapes.

PAULA FOX

I appreciate that there are two sides to this issue,
but I cannot be on both sides at the same time.

JAMES JOYCE, to his publisher when they
were arguing about a manuscript change

Writing and Reading

We would assume that what it was we meant would have been listed in some book set down beyond the sky's far reaches, if at all there was a purpose here. But now I think the purpose lives in us and that we fall into an error if we do not keep our own true notebook of the way we came, how the sleet stung, or how a wandering bird cried at the window. . . .

LOREN EISELEY,
The Lost Notebooks of Loren Eiseley

—

A book should serve as an axe for the frozen sea within us.

FRANZ KAFKA, letter to Oskar Pollak,
in *Letters to Friends, Family and Editors*

—

Women, I believe, search for fellow beings who have faced similar struggles, conveyed them in ways a reader can transform into her own life, confirmed desires the reader had hardly acknowledged—desires that now seem possible. Women catch courage from the women whose lives and writings they read, and women call the bearer of that courage friend.

CAROLYN G. HEILBRUN,
The Last Gift of Time

Writing and Reading

If happiness existed down here, it would be a library.

RENE CHAR

Most collectors of verses and sayings proceed as if they were eating cherries or oysters, choosing the best first, and ending by eating them all.

NICOLAS CHAMFORT,
Products of the Perfected Civilization

People say that life's the thing, but I prefer reading.

LOGAN PEARSALL SMITH,
Afterthoughts

Writing and Reading

Descriptions and Images

Sometimes a vivid image leaps from a page, insisting that I jot it down for my bedside table collection.

The cocktail party—as the name itself indicates—was originally invented by dogs. They are simply bottom-sniffings raised to the rank of formal ceremonies.

LAWRENCE DURRELL, *Justine*

Trying to approach Cate's mind was like trying to walk toward the repellent forces of a magnet.

GAIL GODWIN, *A Mother and Two Daughters*

His character was as thin as a single sheet of gold leaf.

LAWRENCE DURRELL, *Justine*

[He has] a long narrow head and mouth like a malevolent sheep.

Letters: Sylvia Townsend Warner

Her upper lids as green as shutters . . .

WALLACE STEGNER, *Angle of Repose*

Descriptions

Smells are surer than sounds or sights
To make your heart-strings crack —
RUDYARD KIPLING, from "Lichtenberg"

—

The bicyclists rode thirteen times around the town, and
it was ravishing to see them flash past and stream away
down the avenue like a flight of macaws. . . .

Letters: Sylvia Townsend Warner

—

The magnificent music rose in great waves toward that
perfect moment at the end of every piece when there
was silence. SCOTT TUROW, *The Burden of Proof*

—

He [Geoffrey Scott] was tall and dark and had the
distinguished face of a failure.

VIRGINIA WOOLF, *The Diaries of Virginia Woolf*

and Images

Oceans of integrity, puddles of dependability . . .

J. P. DONLEAVY,
The Ginger Man

He will run into any mould, but he won't keep shape.

GEORGE ELIOT,
Middlemarch

Nathan, all the world knows, is by profession a handsome man. MARY CHESNUT, *Mary Chesnut's Civil War*

Reason has moons, but moons not hers
Lie mirrored on her sea,
Confounding her astronomers,
But, oh, delighting me!

RALPH HODGSON,
from "Reason Has Moons"

Descriptions

"But this is something quite new!" said Mrs. Munt,
who collected new ideas as a squirrel collects nuts, and
was especially attracted by those that are portable.

E. M. FORSTER,
Howards End

⬙

I couldn't help wondering if her lamentable lacks, both
secretarial and personal, were her own, or only a mani-
festation of the modern inability to do anything right.

WALLACE STEGNER,
Angle of Repose

⬙

Later she [the Duchess of Devonshire] became the wraith
of what she had been, and still be-wigged and be-diamonded
and be-rouged, she was rather like the half-ruinous shell of
some castellated keep, with the flower boxes in full bloom
on the crumbling sills.   E. F. BENSON

Descriptions

An indescribable confusion [in the studio] with Reynolds
serenely finding whatever it is he wants, like a bumblebee
over a flowerbed.   *Letters: Sylvia Townsend Warner*

—

Sometimes, in my impotence and need I secreted a
venom which infected all my life for days on end and
which spurted out indiscriminately.

MURIEL SPARK, *The Portobello Road*

—

A bitter heart that bides its time and bites.

ROBERT BROWNING, from
"Caliban upon Setebos"

—

Guests from the humbler spheres of life like prostitution
and the arts . . .

LAWRENCE DURRELL, *Justine*

and Images

Happiness and Melancholy

☙ Happiness and melancholy are the heads and tails of the coins of life. Each of us explores these emotions, sometimes trying to understand, sometimes simply trying to absorb, to be there.

Happy as only the truly obsessed can be . . .

ELEANOR PERENYI, *Green Thoughts:*
A Writer in the Garden

∼

Three grand essentials to happiness in this life are something
to do, something to love, and something to hope for.

JOSEPH ADDISON

∼

In the midst of winter I learned that there was in me an
invincible summer.   ALBERT CAMUS, *Actuelles*

∼

How are the waters of the world sweet —if we should die,
we have drunk them. If we should sin —or separate —if
we should fail or succeed —we have tasted of happiness —
we must be written in the book of the blessed.

JOHN JAY CHAPMAN

Happiness

To bless this region, its vendages, and those
Who call it home: though one cannot always
Remember why one has been happy,
There is no forgetting that one was.

W. H. AUDEN, *Good-bye to the Mezzogiorno*

—

If I should ever write to you and complain of my lot, remind
me that in February of 1949 I went with Valentine to Italy.

Letters: Sylvia Townsend Warner

—

I will not wish thee riches, nor the
Glow of greatness, but that wherever thou go
Some weary heart shall gladden at thy smile,
Or shadowed life know sunshine for awhile.
And so thy path shall be a track of light,
Like angels' footsteps passing through the night.

Old English blessing

and Melancholy

The deeper that sorrow carves into your being, the more joy
you can contain.   KAHLIL GIBRAN, *The Prophet*

—

Every moment of genuine joy is recorded in every cell
in your body, along with every moment of hopelessness,
resignation, defeat.   DR. CARL SIMONTON

—

What horror to awake at night
and in the dimness see the light.
Time is white
Mosquitoes bite
I've spent my life on nothing.

Lorine Niedecker: Collected Works

—

The opposite of depression is not happiness but vitality,
and my life, as I write this, is vital, even when it's sad.

ANDREW SOLOMON, "Anatomy of Melancholy"

Happiness

But there is an inner peace nothing can reach; no insult can violate, no corruption can deprave. Hold to that; it is what your childish innocence once was and what your adult maturity must become.

SEAMUS DEANE,
Reading in the Dark

Happiness is the constant striving after some desirable object with a sense of constant progress towards its attainment.

MME. DE STAËL

We cannot help the birds of sadness flying over our heads, but we need not let them build nests in our hair.

Chinese saying

and Melancholy

Loss and Mourning

∽There are many kinds of loss, many kinds of mourning and sadness. Like everyone, I have mourned for people, relationships, and dreams.

I feel uprooted, like a mass of dead seaweed tossed here and there in the waves.　　GUSTAVE FLAUBERT

Grief is different. Grief has no distance. Grief comes in waves, paroxysms, sudden apprehensions that weaken the knees and blind the eyes and obliterate the dailiness of life.

JOAN DIDION,
The Year of Magical Thinking

To mourn is to be eaten alive with homesickness for the person.　　OLIVE ANN BURNS, *Cold Sassy Tree*

The birds sing, but they have no song that I can hear.

BERYL MARKHAM,
West with the Night

Loss and

There is no good arguing with the inevitable. The only argument available with an East Wind is to put on your overcoat.   DENYS FINCH-HATTON

I shall not see the end of this unweaving.
I shall lie dead in any narrow ditch
Before they are unwoven, love and grieving,
And our lives separated, stitch by stitch.
I shall be dead before this task is done,
Not for a moment give you your cool head.
Say we had twenty years and now have none.
Are you Old Fate itself to snap the thread,
And to cut both your life and mine in half
Before the whole design is written clear?
This tapestry will not unweave itself,
Nor I spend what is left of me to tear
Your bright thread out; let unfulfilled design
Stand as your tragic epitaph, and mine.

MAY SARTON,
from "A Divorce of Lovers"

Mourning

It is said that grace enters the soul through a wound.

HEATHER MCDONALD, An Almost Holy Picture

⬦

Hecuba lies there
Before the gates. She weeps
Many tears for many griefs.
And one still hidden from her.

EURIPIDES, from The Trojan Women

⬦

A single person is missing for you, and the whole world
is empty.

PHILIPPE ARIES,
Western Attitudes Toward Death

⬦

Departing then — forever —
Forever — until May —
Forever is deciduous —
Except to those who die —

EMILY DICKINSON, from
"Summer has two Beginnings"

Loss and

And she laughed, sitting there in her mourning, laughed her shrill, young girl's laugh, clapping her hands with delight at the kitten. Then, of a sudden, searing memory stemmed that brilliant cascade and dried the tears of laughter in my mother's eyes. Yet she offered no excuse for having laughed, either on that day or on the days that followed; for though she had lost the man she passionately loved, in her kindness for us she remained among us just as she had always been, accepting her sorrow as she would have accepted the advent of a long and dreary season, but welcoming from every source the fleeting benediction of joy. So she lived on, swept by shadow and sunshine, bowed by bodily torments, resigned, unpredictable and generous, rich in children, flowers and animals like a fruitful domain.

COLETTE, about her mother

We loved the earth, but could not stay.

Old saying, quoted by
Jim Harrison in *Dalva*

Mourning

They shall not grow old, as we that are left grow old:
Age shall not weary them, nor the years condemn.
At the going down of the sun and in the morning
We will remember them.

LAURENCE BINYON, from "For the Fallen"

People imagine that missing a loved one is kind of like
missing cigarettes. The first day is really hard but the next
day is less hard and so forth, easier and easier the longer
you go on. But instead it's like missing water. Every day
you notice the person's absence more.

ANNE TYLER, *Back When We Were Grownups*

Ah, cannot the curled shoots of the larkspur that you
    loved so,
Cannot the spiny poppy that no winter kills
Instruct you how to return through the thawing ground
    and the thin snow
Into this April sun that is driving the mist between the hills?

Loss and

A good friend to the monkshood in a time of need
You were, and the lupine's friend as well;
But I see the lupine lift the ground like a tough weed
And the earth over the monkshood swell,

And I fear that not a root in all this heaving sea
Of land, has nudged you where you lie, has found
Patience and time to direct you, numb and stupid as you
    still must be
From your first winter underground.

EDNA ST. VINCENT MILLAY,
"Spring in the Garden," about her mother

The death of a parent, despite our preparation, indeed,
despite our age, dislodges things deep in us, sets off reactions
that surprise us and that may cut free memories and feelings
that we thought gone to ground long ago. We might, in that
indeterminate period they call mourning, be in a submarine,
silent on the ocean's bed, aware of the depth charges, now
near and now far, buffeting us with recollections.

JOAN DIDION, *The Year of Magical Thinking*

Mourning

And when he died, he died so swift
His death was like a final gift
He went out when the tide was full
Still undiminished, bountiful.

MAY SARTON, from "A Celebration
for George Sarton," about her father

The bustle in a house
The morning after death
Is solemnest of industries
Enacted upon earth, —

The sweeping up the heart,
And putting love away
We shall not want to use again
Until eternity.

EMILY DICKINSON,
"The bustle in a house"

Loss and

Grant that I may seek rather to comfort than to be
comforted. . . .   SAINT FRANCIS OF ASSISI

—

There are the living still to work for, while mourning for
the dead.   ROSE FITZGERALD KENNEDY,
Times to Remember

—

They still live on earth in the acts of goodness they
performed and in the hearts of those who cherish their
memory.   *The Union Prayer Book*

—

That which had been too terrible to be fully faced, even in
imagination, had happened in reality. Now nothing more
could come; by being utterly bereft, she was secure.

IRIS ORIGO, *Allegra*

Mourning

If I can let you go as trees let go
Their leaves, so casually, one by one;
If I can come to know what they do know,
That fall is the release, the consummation,
Then fear of time and the uncertain fruit
Would not distemper the great lucid skies
This strangest autumn, mellow and acute.
If I can take the dark with open eyes
And call it seasonal, not harsh or strange
(For love itself may need a time of sleep),
And, treelike, stand unmoved before the change,
Lose what I lose to keep what I can keep.
The strong root still alive under the snow,
Love will endure—if I can let you go.

MAY SARTON, from "The Autumn Sonnets"

My wind is turned to bitter north
That was so soft a south before. . . .

ARTHUR HUGH CLOUGH,
from "A Song of Autumn"

Loss and

And can it be that in a world so full and busy, the loss
of one weak creature makes a void in any heart so wide
and deep. . . .   CHARLES DICKENS,
                                          Dombey and Son

Pain and beauty are again woven together in my mind,
unbearably, this spring.
                         ANNE MORROW LINDBERGH,
                            Hour of Gold, Hour of Lead

Barn's burnt down —
now
I can see the moon.

                                          MASAHIDE

Mourning

Life

⸙ This section is longer than most of the others because I have found that the subject stretches amiably to accommodate a variety of treasures.

One life is an absurdly small allowance.

FREYA STARK, from *Letters, Volume 1:*
The Furnace and the Cup, 1914–1930

I have three entire days alone — three pure and rounded pearls.

VIRGINIA WOOLF

Bills, business, notes, telephone, and the usual endless petrifying drip of little things . . .

EDITH WHARTON,
letter to Bernard Berenson

Always to be doing more than one wished and less than one ought.

JANE AUSTEN,
Emma

Life

I arise in the morning torn between the desire to improve the world and a desire to enjoy the world. This makes it hard to plan the day.

E. B. WHITE

I was just able to crawl up and down my daily life, nothing more.

Letters: Sylvia Townsend Warner

Her life was as cold as a garret whose windows face north, and boredom like a spider spun its web in all the corners of her heart.

GUSTAVE FLAUBERT, *Madame Bovary*

He had no itch to get to the truth of a story, frankly preferring its most picturesque form.

EVELYN WAUGH, writing about his father in *A Little Learning*

Life

Much madness is divinest sense
To a discerning eye;
Much sense the starkest madness.
'T is the majority
In this, as all, prevails.
Assent, and you are sane;
Demur, —you 're straightway dangerous,
And handled with a chain.

EMILY DICKINSON,
"Much madness is divinest sense"

⚊

Memory is a complicated thing, a relative to truth, but not
its twin.   BARBARA KINGSOLVER, *Animal Dreams*

⚊

The actual and the imaginary may meet and each imbue
itself with a sense of the other. . . .

NATHANIEL HAWTHORNE, *The Scarlet Letter*

Life

How could you tear yourself away from Cahors just when
the autumn crocuses must be coming out in those meadows?
Yet I who ask it saw them and was torn on, though I have
seldom left a town with more regret. It is insane how one
is dragged through life as if through a hedge backwards,
leaving tufts of bloodied wool on every thorn tree.

Letters: Sylvia Townsend Warner

Habit had come to take me in her arms and carry me all the
way up to my bed like a little child.

MARCEL PROUST, *Swann's Way*

Actual life is full of false clues and sign-posts that lead
nowhere. With infinite effort we nerve ourselves for the cri-
sis that never comes. The most successful career must show
a waste of strength that might have removed mountains,
and the most unsuccessful is not that of a man who is taken
unprepared but of him who has prepared and is never taken.

E. M. FORSTER, *Howards End*

$\mathcal{L}ife$

As flies to wanton boys, are we to the gods;
They kill us for their sport.

WILLIAM SHAKESPEARE, *King Lear*

❧

Crucifixion can be discussed philosophically until they start
driving the nails.

WALLACE STEGNER,
The Spectator Bird

❧

This series of tragedies . . . accounted for Woolf's sense
of precariousness, her awareness of the menace lurking
beneath tranquility.

JULIA BRIGGS,
Virginia Woolf: An Inner Life

❧

You can never tell where rescue is going to come from,
or where and in what shape it's going to leave you when
it goes away again.

JANET HOBHOUSE, *The Furies*

❧

The moon affects the tide and the untied.

ANNE WASHINGTON BLAGDEN,
in conversation

Life

The fragrance always remains in the hand that gives
the rose.   HEDA BEJAR

⟋

So it was either a miracle . . . or maybe it was more of a gift,
one that required some assembly.

ANNE LAMOTT, *Traveling Mercies*

⟋

I have sometimes thought that a woman's nature is like a
great house full of rooms: there is the hall, through which
everyone passes going in and out; the drawing room where
one receives formal visits; the sitting room, where members
of the family come and go as they list; but beyond that, far
beyond, are other rooms, the handles of whose doors perhaps are never turned; no one knows the way to them, no
one knows whither they lead; and in the innermost room,
the holy of holies, the soul sits alone and waits for a footstep
that never comes.   EDITH WHARTON,
"The Fullness of Life"

Life

Life is a thing so exquisite that everything conspires to break it. EMILY DICKINSON, *Letters*

➤

As it appeared to me, a practising physician, life would provide all the discomfort anybody needed, without making a principle of it. ROBERTSON DAVIES, *The Cunning Man*

➤

If one must die, he thought, and clearly one must, I can die. But I hate it. ERNEST HEMINGWAY, *For Whom the Bell Tolls*

➤

I am turning over a new leaf but the page is stuck.

DIANE ARBUS

Life

Growing Old

⚬❦⚬ If we are fortunate to live long enough, growing old, like other chapters in life, presents interesting challenges and opportunities. I have looked to various writers for help in understanding and adapting to this stage, or in choosing not to adapt, as in "Rage, rage against the dying of the light." ⚬❦⚬ ⚬❦⚬ ⚬❦⚬ ⚬❦⚬ ⚬❦⚬

Old age came upon me as a surprise, like a frost.

ELIZABETH I

Sixty-four sounded to her like some other person's age.

ANNE TYLER,
The Amateur Marriage

What I object to is the steady process of gradual dilapidation: now it's the knees, then the back, and in my case the eyes. In the new system I propose we would all go vigorously full speed ahead until our time was up, then fall suddenly on our faces, finished. Montaigne, the essayist, said he hoped Death would find him planting cabbages. I myself would like to meet Death in the flower garden — falling face down onto a cushion of *dianthus gratianapolitanus*, if it's not too much to ask.

ELISABETH SHELDON,
Time and the Gardener

Growing Old

Beautiful young people are accidents of nature, but beautiful old people are works of art.

ELEANOR ROOSEVELT

Time and trouble will tame an advanced young woman, but an advanced old woman is uncontrollable by any earthly force. DOROTHY L. SAYERS

The major danger in one's sixties — so I came to feel — is to be trapped in one's body and one's habits, not to recognize those supposedly sedate years as the time to discover new choices and to act upon them. To continue doing what one had been doing — which was Dante's idea of hell — is, I came to see, and the vision frightened me, easy in one's sixties.

CAROLYN G. HEILBRUN,
The Last Gift of Time

Growing Old

There is only one solution if old age is not to be an absurd parody of our former life, and that is to go on pursuing ends that give our existence a meaning—devotion to individuals, to groups or to causes, social, political, intellectual or creative work. In spite of the moralists' opinion to the contrary, in old age we should wish still to have passions strong enough to prevent us turning in on ourselves.

SIMONE DE BEAUVOIR, *The Coming of Age*

After sixty one's rule should be never to waste time over things one doesn't want.   FREYA STARK

After forty a man denies himself no reasonable and harmless indulgence; he has learned by that time that it is a pity and a folly to do so.   WILLIAM D. HOWELLS, *Indian Summer*

What a wonderful life I've had—I only wish I had realized it sooner.   COLETTE

Growing Old

What is so nice and so unexpected about life is the way it improves as it goes along. I think you should impress this fact on your children because I think young people have an awful feeling that life is slipping past them and they must do something—catch something—they don't quite know what, whereas they've only got to wait—it all comes.

NANCY MITFORD, letter to Evelyn Waugh

We are all happier in many ways when we are old than when we were young. The young sow wild oats, the old grow sage.

WINSTON CHURCHILL

I made hay while the sun shone.
My work sold.
Now, if the harvest is over
And the world cold,
Give me the bonus of laughter
As I lose hold.

JOHN BETJEMAN, "The Last Laugh"

Growing Old

In their mid to late forties, they felt the malaise of that period no deeper than other men but were considerably more dramatic about it than all but a few.

JIM HARRISON, *Julip*

But right now, with all his passions somehow turning like the tide towards yearnings of loss rather than hungers for gain . . .

PETER POUNCEY,
Rules for Old Men Waiting

As we neared our sixties the cloaks we had wrapped about our essential selves were wearing thin.

ROBERTSON DAVIES, *Fifth Business*

When I was young I got my emotion from having things done to me . . . by art or love or by eloquence; now, by doing things myself.

The Diaries of Sylvia Townsend Warner

Growing Old

Gardening is one of the rewards of middle age, when one
is ready for an impersonal passion, a passion that demands
patience, acute awareness of a world outside oneself, and the
power to keep on growing through all the times of drought,
through the cold snows, toward those moments of pure joy
when all failures are forgotten and the plum tree flowers.

MAY SARTON, *Plant Dreaming Deep*

And she knew that she neared the end of the garden path
And the deer and the buried candles travelled with her
But still she knew that she would not make an end
Of setting her plants before the shroud came round her. . . .

VITA SACKVILLE-WEST, from "The Garden"

Do not go gentle into that good night,
Old age should burn and rave at close of day;
Rage, rage against the dying of the light.

DYLAN THOMAS, from "Do Not Go
Gentle into That Good Night"

Growing Old

Nature

The natural world provides a framework, a sense of place in which we can locate ourselves. Its varied beauty is a welcome bonus.

The wonder of the world, the beauty and the power, the shape of things, their colors, lights and shades; these I saw. Look ye also while life lasts.

Gravestone in Cumberland, England

In the highlands you woke up in the morning and thought: Here I am where I ought to be.

ISAK DINESEN, *Out of Africa*

The way a crow
Shook down on me
A drift of snow
From a hemlock tree

Has given my heart
A change of mood
And saved some part
Of a day I had rued.

ROBERT FROST, "Dust of Snow"

Nature

In beauty, may I walk
On the trail marked with pollen, may I walk
With grasshoppers about my feet, may I walk
With dew about my feet, may I walk
With beauty, may I walk
With beauty before me
With beauty behind me
With beauty above me
May I walk

Anonymous, from the Navajo

Everything that seems empty is full of the angels of God.

SAINT HILARY,
fourth century A.D.

Woe to those who join house to house, who add field to
field until there is not a place where they may be alone.

ISAIAH

Nature

In my book a pioneer is a man who turned all the grass upside down, strung bob-wire over the dust that was left, poisoned the water and cut down the trees, killed the Indian who owned the land and called it progress. If I had my way the land here would be like God made it, and none of you sons of bitches would be here at all.

CHARLES RUSSELL

~

The world today is sick to its thin blood for lack of elemental things, for fire before the hands, for water welling from the earth, for air, for the dear earth itself underfoot.

HENRY BESTON,
The Outermost House

~

If such a phenomenon occurred but once, it would be handed down by tradition to posterity, and get into the mythology at last.   HENRY DAVID THOREAU, *Walden*,
on fall foliage in New England

Nature

Here I sit looking out on snow and ice and a blue sky.
The children are sledging, and the furry brown hedgerow,
all withered and unkempt, looks on like a kind dog.

Letters: Sylvia Townsend Warner

⌣

What would the world be, once bereft
Of wet and of wildness? Let them be left,
O let them be left, wildness and wet;
Long live the weeds and the wilderness yet.

GERARD MANLEY HOPKINS, from "Inversnaid"

⌣

The north wind is raving, and the air is bruised and black.

Letters: Sylvia Townsend Warner

⌣

Had I the heavens' embroidered cloths,
Enwrought with golden and silver light,
The blue and the dim and the dark cloths
Of night and light and the half light . . .

WILLIAM BUTLER YEATS, from
"Aedh wishes for the Cloths of Heaven"

Nature

The animals shall not be measured by man. In a world older and more complete than ours, they move finished and complete, gifted with extensions of the senses we have lost or never attained, living by voices we shall never hear. They are not brethren, they are not underlings: they are other nations, caught with ourselves in the net of life, fellow prisoners of the splendor and travail of the earth.

HENRY BESTON, *The Outermost House*

Whatever peace I know rests in the natural world, in feeling myself a part of it, even in a small way.

MAY SARTON, *Journal of a Solitude*

Every day this May ere thou dine:
Go look upon the fresh daisy,
And, though thou be for woe in point to die,
That shall full greatly less thee of thy pine.

GEOFFREY CHAUCER, from
"The Cuckoo and the Nightingale"

Nature

Nature's first green is gold,
Her hardest hue to hold.
Her early leaf's a flower;
But only so an hour.
Then leaf subsides to leaf.
So Eden sank to grief,
So dawn goes down to day.
Nothing gold can stay.

ROBERT FROST, "Nothing Gold Can Stay"

Thank heavens the sun has gone in and I don't have to
go out and enjoy it.   LOGAN PEARSALL SMITH

And since to look at things in bloom
Fifty springs are little room,
About the woodlands I will go
To see the cherry hung with snow.

A. E. HOUSMAN, from *A Shropshire Lad*

Nature

The bluebird carries the sky on his back.

HENRY DAVID THOREAU,
Journal, April 3, 1852

Glory be to God for dappled things —
For skies of couple-colour as a brinded cow;
For rose-moles all in stipple upon trout that swim;
Fresh-firecoal chestnut-falls; finches' wings; . . .

GERARD MANLEY HOPKINS,
from "Pied Beauty"

I have been one acquainted with the night.
I have walked out in rain — and back in rain.

ROBERT FROST, from
"Acquainted with the Night"

Nature

... Earth's crammed with heaven,
And every common bush afire with God;
But only he who sees, takes off his shoes,
The rest sit round it, and pluck blackberries ...

ELIZABETH BARRETT BROWNING,
from "Aurora Leigh"

I hadn't been expecting to see my first albatross until later,
on Hood Island, where they nest. But in an abrupt clearing
of the mist and driving rain, there it was, drifting low over
the ragged sea. Enormous and powerful, effortless as sleep,
it crossed our wake and then was gone in another squall.
While some would say this was merely luck, others might
call it grace.

Suddenly any memory of whatever I might have learned
about the albatross seemed irrelevant. It was enough to have
seen it at that moment, and I was left with an enchanted
sense that I had received a gift.

GRAEME GIBSON, *The Bedside Book of Birds*

Nature

Travel

⌒∞⌒ Many good writers have written about their travels, and certainly many good readers enjoy reading about travel. I do love to travel, but in the case of expeditions to places such as Afghanistan, Sri Lanka, or New Guinea, I much prefer reading about other people's adventures.

Travel is fatal to prejudice, bigotry and narrow-mindedness.

MARK TWAIN, *The Innocents Abroad*

—

The drawback to a journey that has been too well planned
is that it does not leave enough room for adventure.

ANDRÉ GIDE

—

For all my worries about not understanding enough, about
being deceived by surface reality, about not seeing through
to the truth of whatever I happen to be observing, still there
are moments—whole days—of constant surprise, of enjoy-
ment and happiness so pure that I'm content to exist in
the moment and on the surface.   FRANCINE PROSE,
Sicilian Odyssey

—

Still the world is wondrous large, — seven seas from marge
      to marge, —
And it holds a vast of various kinds of man;
And the wildest dreams of Kew are the facts of
      Khatmandhu . . .

RUDYARD KIPLING, from "In the Neolithic Age"

Travel

My main aim in going to Congo Français was to get up
above the tide line of the Ogowé River and there collect
fishes; . . . This is a fascinating pursuit. But it is a pleasure
to be indulged in with caution; for one thing, you are certain
to come across crocodiles.

MARY KINGSLEY,
Travels in West Africa, 1894

We are back — except for the part of me which has stayed
in Provence. It seemed blasphemy to come away from a
place where I was so entirely happy.

Letters: Sylvia Townsend Warner

My presentiment of the emotions with which I should
behold the Roman ruins has proved quite correct.

Excerpt from an
eighteenth-century guidebook

Travel

House and Home

Wherever I have lived, my house has been important to me. Comfort and beautiful things around me, perhaps a view of distant hills, all provide me with a sense of happiness and ease.

One had to find out what things were not necessary, what things one really needed. A little music and liquor, still less food, a warm and beautiful but not too big roof of one's own, a channel for one's creative energies and love, the sun and the moon.

T. H. WHITE,
The Goshawk

A person's life is not a series of dramatic events for which he or she is applauded or exiled but a slow accumulation of days, seasons, years, fleshed out by the generational weight of one's family and anchored by a land-bound sense of place.

GRETEL EHRLICH,
The Solace of Open Spaces

I don't want to own all the land in the world, only those bits that border on mine.

Author unknown

House and Home

A kitchen stove is so made that it drops its coals and tells you, with every fall, that life burns away, and it has the stove top for a kettle to remind you that there is always tea, and that the best comforts are at everyone's hand.

JOYCE CARY,
The Horse's Mouth

It seems to me that our three basic needs, for food and security and love, are so mixed and mingled and entwined that we cannot straightly think of one without the others.... There is a communion of more than our bodies when bread is broken and wine drunk.

M.F.K. FISHER, *The Art of Eating*

Building is an enjoyable way of getting poorer.

LUCA PITTI,
fifteenth century

House and Home

Art, Taste, and Style

Connoisseurs, philistines—all of us know what we like—but exactly why something appeals is an interesting question. Although one can and should work to train one's eye, an element of the personal inevitably becomes part of the process.

Everyone carries his own inch-rule of taste and amuses himself by applying it, triumphantly, wherever he travels.

HENRY ADAMS,
The Education of Henry Adams

❧

I want my living room to look like a garden, a garden in hell.

DIANA VREELAND

❧

Good taste is really just a kind of aesthetic vegetarianism.

ROBERTSON DAVIES, *The Lyre of Orpheus*

❧

The contemplation of things as they are, without error or confusion, without substitution or imposture, is in itself a nobler thing than a whole harvest of invention.

FRANCIS BACON—a quotation Dorothea Lange pinned to her darkroom door

Art, Taste,

Insofar as photography does peel away the dry wrappers of habitual seeing, it creates another habit of seeing: both intense and cool, solicitous and detached; charmed by the insignificant detail, addicted to incongruity.

SUSAN SONTAG, *On Photography*

＊

I work in the garden, I look at the flowers and shrubs and trees and discover in them an exquisiteness of contour, a vitality of edge or a vigor of spring as well as an infinite variety of color that no artifact I have seen in the last sixty years can rival. . . . Each day, as I look, I wonder where my eyes were yesterday.

BERNARD BERENSON

＊

Stare. It is the way to educate your eye, and more. Stare, pry, listen, eavesdrop. Die knowing something. You are not here long.

WALKER EVANS, in *Walker Evans: A Biography*, by Belinda Rathbone

and Style

History and Politics

⟨∞⟩⟨∞⟩ Politics and history are intertwined. Each affects the way one thinks about the other. Croesus, Emerson, Goebbels, and Will Rogers all influence the way I read the *New York Times* or a history or biography. ⟨∞⟩ ⟨∞⟩ ⟨∞⟩ ⟨∞⟩

Sometimes I wonder whether the world is being run by smart people who are putting us on or by imbeciles who really mean it.

MARK TWAIN

◆

It was, after all, the Greeks who pioneered the writing of history as what it has so largely remained, an exercise in political ironics — an intelligible story of how men's actions produce results other than those they intended.

J.G.A. POCOCK

◆

Later somebody can sit around for days and weeks and figure out how things might have been done differently. This is all very well and very interesting and quite irrelevant.

GEORGE ELSEY, on the Marshall Plan
and the Truman Doctrine

◆

Chaos is the law of nature, order is the dream of man.

HENRY ADAMS, *The Education of Henry Adams*

History

Much of foreign policy is about nuances that can be lost
on the public, and perhaps on the intended recipients.
The policymakers can take such pains over finding just
the right word that they assume others will attach as much
importance to the word as they do.

ELIZABETH DREW,
in *The New Yorker*

Suggested epitaph for a diplomat: His mediocrity was his
salvation.   LAWRENCE DURRELL, *Justine*

Policy is like a play in many acts which unfold inexorably
once the curtain is raised. To declare then that the perfor-
mance will not go on is an absurdity. The play will be
completed either by the actors or by the spectators who
mount the stage.

KLEMENS WENZEL VON METTERNICH

and Politics

Those that would give up essential liberty to gain a little temporary safety deserve neither liberty nor safety.

BENJAMIN FRANKLIN

A ship in the harbor is safe, but then again that is not what ships are built for.

Author unknown

He is brilliant but corrupt, like a dead mackerel by moonlight, which shines and stinks.

AARON BURR, describing a
contemporary political figure

His native strength . . . compelled every man to be his tool that came within his reach; and the more cunning the man, the sharper the tool—the more uncompromising the man, the better tool he would be for the making of compromises.

NATHANIEL HAWTHORNE, on Andrew Jackson

History

Everybody in fine spirits. They have one and all spoken in the Congress to their own perfect satisfaction.

MARY CHESNUT,
Mary Chesnut's Civil War

You can always depend on the American people to do the right thing—once they've explored all the other possibilities.

WINSTON CHURCHILL

Though Parisians believe that they are superior by birth, they do not believe, as Americans do, that they are invulnerable by right. ADAM GOPNIK,
Paris to the Moon

A tyrant is always setting some war in motion so that the people will be in need of a leader. PLATO

and Politics

Why of course the people don't want war. But it is the leaders who determine policy, and it is always a simple matter to drag the people along. All you have to do is tell them they are being attacked, and denounce the peacemakers for lack of patriotism and exposing the country to danger. It works the same in any country.　　　　JOSEPH GOEBBELS
(Hitler's Minister for Popular
Enlightenment and Propaganda)

In war the fathers bury their sons, whereas in peace the sons bury their fathers.　　　　CROESUS

I have seen much war in my lifetime and I hate it profoundly. But there are worse things than war; and all of them come with defeat.

ERNEST HEMINGWAY, *Men at War*

O God that madest this beautiful earth, when will it be ready to receive thy saints? How long, O Lord, how long?

GEORGE BERNARD SHAW, *Saint Joan*

History

Where there is truth there is no peace, and where there is peace there is no truth.

Old rabbinical saying

~

It is the absolute right of the State to supervise the formation of public opinion.   JOSEPH GOEBBELS

~

The rank and file are usually much more primitive than we imagine. Propaganda must therefore always be essentially simple and repetitious.   JOSEPH GOEBBELS

~

If you tell a lie big enough and keep repeating it, people will eventually come to believe it.   JOSEPH GOEBBELS

~

Same old pile of crap, just a new swarm of flies.

WILL ROGERS

and Politics

Endorsing God and implying that God returns the
compliment . . .   EUGENE J. MCCARTHY

Whoever fights monsters should see to it that in the process
he does not become a monster.

FRIEDRICH NIETZSCHE

When you strike at a king, you must kill him.

RALPH WALDO EMERSON

Power is like a snake. When you try to hand it over to
someone, one of the two of you is bound to get bitten.

OMAR TORRIJOS

I am the kind of conservative who looks into the bathwater
to see if there's a baby in there.   MICHAEL THOMAS

History

We suffer from a sleeping sickness of the soul, the feeling that we lack at some core level meaning in our individual lives, and meaning collectively, that sense that our lives are part of some greater effort, that we are connected to one another. . . . Let us be willing to remold society by redefining what it means to be a human being.

HILLARY RODHAM CLINTON

A society so hidebound and ingrown that it treated the imminent collapse of western civilization as an unwarranted intrusion on its own comfort.

HILARY SPURLING, *Paul Scott*

All I wanted was compliance with my wishes after a reasonable period of discussion.

WINSTON CHURCHILL

Society, too, human society is like a stew—if you don't stir it up, the scum stays on top. EDWARD ABBEY

and Politics

Advice for Living

❧ I have always been drawn to proverbs and other pithy words of advice on how one should live, how one should behave. ❧ ❧ ❧

When shall we live, if not now?

SENECA

—

Things won are done; joy's soul lies in the doing.

WILLIAM SHAKESPEARE,
Troilus and Cressida

—

Don't try to teach a pig to sing. It wastes time and only annoys the pig.

Author unknown

—

One of the secrets of a happy life is continuous small treats.

IRIS MURDOCH,
The Sea, the Sea

Advice for Living

Small things can often make big things bearable.

KUKI GALLMANN,
I Dreamed of Africa

—

No bird soars too high if he soars with his own wings.

WILLIAM BLAKE

—

I learned what every dreaming child needs to know—that no horizon is so far you cannot get above it or beyond it. . . .

BERYL MARKHAM,
West with the Night

—

Don't die guessing.

BROOKE ASTOR, quoting her mother

Advice for Living

I salute you.

There is nothing I can give you which you have not; but there is much that, while I cannot give, you can take.

No heaven can come to us unless our hearts find rest in it. Take heaven.

No peace lies in the future which is not hidden in this present instant. Take peace.

The gloom of the world is but a shadow; behind it, yet within our reach, is joy. Take joy.

And so, at this Christmas time, I greet you with the prayer that for you, now and forever, the day breaks and the shadows flee away.

FRA GIOVANNI, 1513 A.D.

Advice for Living

Bashfulness . . . a form of vanity, the only difference being that vanity is the tendency to overestimate your worth, and bashfulness to underestimate it; both arising from the overindulgence of self-consciousness.

E. B. WHITE, diary

—

I'm not telling you to make the world better, because I don't think that progress is necessarily part of the package, I'm just telling you to live in it. To look at it. To try to get the picture. To live recklessly. To take chances. To make your own work and take pride in it. To seize the moment. And if you ask me why you should bother to do that, I could tell you that the grave's a fine and private place, but none I think do there embrace. Nor do they sing there, or write, or argue, or see the tidal bore on the Amazon, or touch their children. And that's what there is to do and get it while you can and good luck at it.

JOAN DIDION,
commencement address,
University of California Riverside, 1975

Advice for Living

Many have sought light and truth, but they sought it outside themselves, where it is not.   SAINT AUGUSTINE

Be kind, for everyone you meet is fighting a great battle.

PHILO OF ALEXANDRIA

Insanity is doing the same thing over and over, each time expecting a different result.   ALBERT EINSTEIN

To be noted is perhaps the most important and least recognized need of the human soul.   SIMONE WEIL

A narcissist is someone who doesn't always listen as closely to you as you think he should.

Author unknown

Advice for Living

In business, as in life, you don't get what you deserve, you get what you negotiate.

CHESTER L. KARRASS,
The Negotiating Game

⬤

Quit being such a puritan, file the point off the prick of conscience. . . .

WALLACE STEGNER,
The Spectator Bird

⬤

A filthy mind is a perpetual feast.

OSBERT LANCASTER

⬤

Solitude is the richness of self, and loneliness is the poverty of self.

MAY SARTON, in a National
Public Radio interview

Advice for Living

Let tomorrow come tomorrow.

ALICE STEINBACH, *Without Reservations*

⬎

One must resign oneself to being a nuisance if one wants to get anything done.   FREYA STARK

⬎

A useless life is an early death.

JOHANN WOLFGANG VON GOETHE

⬎

This is not a dress rehearsal.

DAN LUFKIN, in conversation

⬎

The reasonable man adapts himself to the world; the unreasonable one persists in trying to adapt the world to himself. Therefore, all progress depends on the unreasonable man.

GEORGE BERNARD SHAW, *Man and Superman*

Advice for Living

Any woman who is sure of her own wits is a match, at any time, for a man who is not sure of his own temper.

WILKIE COLLINS, *The Woman in White*

If you're going through hell, keep going.

WINSTON CHURCHILL

The best way out is always through.

ROBERT FROST,
from "A Servant to Servants"

Giants like Karkas—overload them with information and they'll kill you, just to simplify things.

J. K. ROWLING, *Harry Potter and the Order of the Phoenix*

Advice for Living

Don't put it down, put it away.

VIRGINIA WILLIAMS BENTLEY,
Bentley Farm Cookbook

＞

Problem stated at its most succinct: is life too short to be taking shit or is life too short to mind it?

VIOLET WEINGARTEN, *Intimations of Mortality*

＞

Nice is nice to me.

LINCOLN KIRSTEIN, in *Other People's Letters*, by Mina Curtiss

＞

There's no use crying over spilt milk; it only makes it salty for the cat.

Popular wisdom

Advice for Living

Never interrupt your opponent when he is busy committing
suicide.   LEE ATWATER

Never get in a pissing match with a skunk.

Cowboy saying

I don't mind what people do as long as they don't do it in
the street and frighten the horses.

JENNIE JEROME CHURCHILL
(mother of Winston Churchill)

The world breaks everyone and afterwards many are strong
at the broken places.

ERNEST HEMINGWAY,
A Farewell to Arms

Advice for Living

Nothing is so exhilarating as to be shot at, without result.

WINSTON CHURCHILL

He who trembles is not bored.

STENDHAL

My father had the gift of making me believe, and of believing himself, that there is always a new adventure, something waiting to be discovered, if we can only find the time to look for it, and the courage to jump.

KUKI GALLMANN, *I Dreamed of Africa*

You can't be a sorcerer every day.

PABLO PICASSO

Advice for Living

PERMISSIONS

Grateful acknowledgment is made to the following for permission to reprint previously published materials:

Auden, W. H., author: "Good-Bye to the Mezzogiorno." Copyright © 1958 by W. H. Auden, from *Collected Poems by W. H. Auden*. Used by permission of Random House, Inc.

Betjeman, Sir John, author: "The Last Laugh," from *John Betjeman Collected Poems, Enlarged Edition*, compiled by the Earl of Birkenhead. Copyright © 1958, 1962, 1970, 1979 by John Betjeman. Reprinted by permission of John Murray (Publishers) Limited.

Cummings, E. E., author: The lines from "All in green went my love riding," from *Complete Poems: 1904–1962*, by E. E. Cummings, edited by George James Firmage. Copyright © 1923, 1951, 1991 by the Trustees for the E. E. Cummings Trust. Copyright © 1976 by George James Firmage. Used by permission of Liveright Publishing Corporation.

Dickinson, Emily, author: from *The Poems of Emily Dickinson*, Thomas H. Johnson, ed., Cambridge, Mass.: The Belknap Press of Harvard University Press. Copyright © 1951, 1955, 1979, 1983 by the President and Fellows of Harvard College. Reprinted by permission of the publishers and the Trustees of Amherst College.

Frost, Robert, author: "Dust of Snow," "Nothing Gold Can Stay," and excerpt from "Acquainted with the Night," from *The Poetry of Robert Frost*, edited by Edward Connery Lathem. Copyright © 1969 by Henry Holt and Company, LLC. Used by permission of Henry Holt and Company, LLC.

INDEX

⌘

PRODUCED BY
WILSTED & TAYLOR PUBLISHING SERVICES

Project management: Christine Taylor
Production assistance: Drew Patty
Copyediting: Nancy Evans
Proofreading: Melody Lacina
Design and composition: Yvonne Tsang
Printer's devilment: Lillian Marie Wilsted
Typeset in Cochin, Copperplate, and Liberty

Printing and binding by Regal Printing, Ltd.,
Hong Kong, through Stacy and Michael Quinn
of Quinnessentials Books and Printing, Inc.